Vakandsdottir

Paul Waggener

VAKANDIBÓK
A Taufr Of Awakening

by

Paul Waggener

OPWW003

Contents

Part I
Vakandibók
A Taufr of Awakening

Introduction

The Intention of this object you now hold is stated in its title: Vakandi. Its aim is to facilitate an Awakening within its reader, promoting an awareness of things unknown and hidden, and allowing its reader to move into the Wakeful State by bringing his being into balance and strengthening all its parts.

Like one who has been asleep, we all have to begin simply, with routine- we must shake the remnants of the long slumber from ourselves and begin to let the light of day filter in.

The focus and techniques found herein are not unique, per se- they are known and practiced in some form or another in many various areas of spiritual study and stem from a thousand traditions. The difference is that here, the practices are applied directly to the ongoing Work within the framework of the Germanic magical art and are organized and laid out in such a fashion as to promote the full understanding and constant strengthening and harmony of the Soul Complex in all its wondrous and inseparable parts.

This will be achieved in three-fold method: Study, Discipline, Application. It is necessary in order to promote the growth and strength of any area of Self that one first understands it on a basic level through intellectual study. His mind must at the very least have a tenuous grasp on the ideas at hand in order to move further in that direction, which is the second part of this work, Discipline. To continue study in any fashion, the seeker must first discipline himself to a rigorous schedule that he honors even in difficult circumstances. He also uses these disciplines to gain more advanced mastery over himself by using them in a focused manner, applying them in order to reach the higher levels of understanding than simply seeing and hearing.

Foremost, that is what this text is designed to provide: a concise, yet detailed system of disciplines, set forth in an organized and degreed fashion to be used in order. You will see this word, discipline, a great deal, for that is at the root of a strong practice, and the root of a strong individual. Like waking oneself from a deep and comfortable sleep, the Will must be employed to bring oneself from that place of comfort and into an oftentimes harsh and cold realm.

These disciplines are difficult, and deliberately so. They are meant to test the will, the endurance, the body, the mind and so on- and if they were simply done with a few days of lukewarm attempts, they would have no value. This Way is only for the True Seeker, the one who truly desires to Know and to Will, who would break the fetters and tear off the blinders in order to be freed from the blindness and the bondage of opiated comfort and self-deceptive ego feeding.

There is darkness here, and light. Oftentimes, one must walk through the one in order to reach the other. Trust only the voice of overcoming, and silence that liar within you who spits the poison and vitriol of weakness, saying always: "I cannot." Burn this away with holy fire, and leave in its place only the words: I WILL. I AM.

First know your goal, then live it. For to live free and unfettered, man must first discover his Self. If he does not know his true Self, how then can he live a life of Truth as he performs the Great Work of bringing who he is now in line with who he is sacrificing himself to Become? Until he comes to Understand all parts of the Self, he is a ship tossed by the waves of Fear, Confusion and Death.

To discover one's true Self is the first part of this Work- to Become it, the second.

To set about on this voyage of discovery, we must work from Silence and Calm to Ecstasy and Madness. The dizzying heights of Knowing can only be reached by first running the Wolf-road; over hill and plain, field and swamp, until at last we reach that path that leads into the Mountain to our ultimate goal.

There is not one way, but many- and in the realization of that path, we will realize that perceptions of One and Many must give way to the All.

Our obstacles on this road will be great and numerous: Distraction, Fear, Laziness, Delusion, Weakness. Even Power itself will raise itself against us as an enemy if we do not learn its ways and wiles. Adversity is a potent teacher, pain a transitory illusion and loss merely a chosen perception. Our minor defeats will burn away in the face of Eternal Victory, and all oppositions quelled by a Word.

This road requires three things above all others: Nobility, Courage and Sacrifice. If we lack the highmindedness to rise above the crawling blindness of this shadowy world of illusion, then we will simply become a part of that illusion. Our bodies will crumble to dust, and there will be nothing left of us that is Indestructible. If we lack the bravery to remain on this difficult road, we will soon awaken with the bitter ashes of mediocrity filling our mouths, as we look over a bleak expanse of wasted moments at the end of our days. If we haven't the ability to Sacrifice all that we Are for all we can Become, then we will have failed before even setting both feet on the Way-there is no room here for the base and impure.

But, if we Work towards these things, growing them and feeding them with the fruit of our efforts, we begin to destroy our fetters, unshackle ourselves from the enslavement of compulsion and reaction and attain real Freedom. Like the thunderstorm we will fashion ourselves – first through a great and profound Calm as we initiate the process of Self-knowledge and deep awareness. Second, we unleash the roaring might of raw Will, manifesting it in the planes of

Form and Sound. Third, we let the sacred waters wash over us and cleanse our imperfections, feed our roots and grow us into a beautiful thing. Fourth, we return to a place of quiet stillness and perfection and allow the sun to shine through us as our spirits absorb and reflect it for all to see. Fifth, we begin the process anew as the energy of our storming rises again, and we are strengthened and re-created by past action- present being- passing away- becoming once more.

The dedicated magician begins by setting for himself a Discipline – a structured regimen of Work that he will adhere to even if it proves extremely difficult. What follows are many individual disciplines, each corresponding to the Nine Realms of the Soul Complex, designed to be performed in degreed fashion, that is, mastering them one by one- fully reaching the depths of the first discipline before moving on to the second- but it is the province of the adherent in order to use these individual practices to form the framework of his greater Discipline.

For each individual, a different approach may be required, and so it is left up to the individual to decide on the application and order of his practice.

For this reason, the Nine Realms of the Soul Complex are listed and discussed here in no particular order- to begin at any point is to experience simply a moment in time, one point of the great circle that binds.

HUGR

Retreating from the madness Without to the madness Within… to silence, to the place beyond silence.

One exists only in opposites until he destroys that in himself which opposes, and becomes One instead of many.

That hidden place cannot be found by moving forward; it is only for those who can cut away everything that surrounds it, and know its simplicity-it is generating, not generated; at the ends of Illusion it shines like a star in the undying firmament.

Residing there, the Will is known. The Self is discovered. The unrealities of existence are put away forever, and what remains is Truth. Destiny shows her face from behind the veil of desire, revealing the inconsistencies between Man and God- he who seeks and he who is fulfilled, slave and free man, transitory and eternal.

That endless cycle of struggle and striving is broken. The binding chains of birth and death are shattered.

Those strands of being and becoming are severed- set free of form and matter, love and hatred, time, space, and all that meet therein.

Seeking and finding that quiet center within is one of most difficult and rewarding elements of the Work at hand. Until we can silence the ever-moving, restless and fickle flow of thought, running like a frenzied river through our consciousness, always threatening to burst the banks and overflow, we cannot find that calm foundation that we :N:eed to build from. The key to this quiet calm is the regular practice of meditation- a dedication to setting aside that time with which we can simply exist and be, Timelessly and Mindlessly, instead of acting, reacting and living our whole life in past and future, never now.

Eternity exists not in an unending linear idea, but in the moment- each moment- that is occurring now. The ability to exist always in the here and now rather than reliving the past or agonizing over future uncertainties is an Unbinding, a freedom that can be felt while watching a single drop of rain fall forever, or the endlessness known during physical love. This moment, this singularity is the treasure in the Waterfall referred to in the :L: mysteries. The rushing of the waterfall that seems to have no beginning, no end- a roaring that never stops, within which one can find total silence. This is the goal of meditation, then: to find that Eternal Moment inside ourselves and to remain there. Unharnessing the Yoke of Time-destroying the concept of existence on a linear plane, here beginning and here ending, so that we are able to realize our own timelessness.

Our day to day life is filled with distraction, noise, unwanted interruption and distractions or interactions. We have become stressed, fearful and anxious about these things, and our fear manifests itself in ways unhealthy to us: substance abuse, co-dependence, obsessive or compulsive behaviors and generally self-destructive practices that we have given power over our own lives. Our fear often comes from the nagging question: Will I have enough? Enough time, enough money, enough affection, the list goes ever on. These often deep-rooted habits and anxieties go unnoticed by the average individual, plaguing their life and dictating their every action, for the simple reason that they have not recognized and admitted the issue to themselves. For how can they know themselves or their deeper impulses when they have never taken the time to do so?

Most human beings know themselves on a cursory level, or rather, they are familiar only with the person that they choose to think they are. They take desirable qualities and attribute these to themselves regardless of their truth, and take great offense if someone suggests that this might not be so. The underlying problem with this is not because it is desirous to throw the hands up in defeat and say: "I am lazy," or "I am deceitful," because Words have power and when we label ourselves as something, we become rooted in that assessment. Rather, it is important to recognize them so we can begin to combat our negative traits in a straightforward fashion, untwisting branches and purifying the Self, so that we might come to say, "Each day I am becoming more motivated and effective," or , "I am becoming more truthful," and so on.

We can see that at root, this cannot be accomplished without meditation and honest self-awareness, allowing a full understanding and recognition of the person we actually are at this moment, instead of the person we would like to think we are. Throughout this process, it is important to remember, we are living in the now, not past or future- each moment we are becoming. We are not "stuck in our ways" or "too old to change now"- this is that fear based thinking of "not enough time." There is enough time because we are living in the endless Now- not in the unknown and non-existent future. We are ever-flowing, ever-changing, ever-becoming, ever-growing, and it is completely our own decision (and no one else's) how we do so.

HUGR DISCIPLINES

I. FORGING THE WONDROUS ITEMS

Setting aside at least 30 minutes daily, the magician creates and sustains Wondrous Items. In a threefold fashion, three times, the magician chooses and forms objects within the hugauga (mind eye). This should begin as a simple meditative work- basic shapes, first, then the second three should be more complex objects that correspond to that shape with added dimension and so on, while the third time through calls for an even more difficult process. For example, for three days, the magician meditates on the following sequence of shapes, one each day: Circle, Square, Triangle, of any color he chooses. The second time, he works with sphere, cube, pyramid. The third, he perfectly constructs a skull, a jewelry box, and a sentinel pine. In this way, he pushes himself more and more to not only create new things, but to draw correspondences between shapes, objects and function. This Discipline should be adhered to for no less than one third of a year. If it proves too difficult to advance to the more complex levels of the discipline in the 3 days allotted, one can instead remain on each 3rd for nine days instead.

II. WALKING THE PATHWAY OF FIRE

The Magician performs the Pathways of Fire Discipline, choosing (or creating, although it is recommended that he begin with staves of a more simple nature, or those already well known to him.) 3 varying galdrastafir with which to do the work. The Discipline is explained below, and should be performed daily for no less than the remaining two thirds of the year.

Here begins the practice of assimilating and internalizing the energies and vital might of the galdrastafir through the method of Entrance and Movement. This is a technique that requires a great deal of practice and a prior experience with visualization work on which to base it- the amount of deep concentration it takes can be developed only through constant meditation and use of exercises mentioned previously- this is not an "entry level" point and should not be taken as such. Frustration with and thwarted attempts to See, Enter and Traverse indicate lack of foundation in these other areas and should be accepted as a lesson, rather than breeding lack of confidence or disheartening the individual.

To begin with, one should select a galdr stave with which he is familiar, whether of his own creation or another's, but it should be one well-worked and Understood. Because the initial experience will deal mainly with familiarizing oneself with the general technique and seeing the stave in a new way, it is beneficial to start with a stave easilly brought into the hugauga. After becoming more proficient, one can explore other areas of this practice at Will.

Bring the symbol into the hugauga. Do this carefully and systematically, first by viewing the entirety of it from without, or above, much as one views it if it is written on paper. However, instead of seeing it as simple lines in ink, see the lines as they are brought into mind, draw them with fire smoothly on a black background, piece by piece in a flowing fashion until the whole symbol is complete, perfect and aflame.

For the purposes of future practice, you must view each single line of the stave as twofold- a going and a coming, if you will, a send and return line, appearing as a simple doubling as if you were drawing each line with two pens held directly parallel with one another. Do this several times, drawing and redrawing-bringing the whole stave to completion, holding it for some time, then erasing it from the end point back to the beginning and starting over. Just doing this will occupy the practitioner for some time, days, weeks, even months, as he develops his ability to line and hold shapes much more complex then the rune-staves he has grown accustomed to.

After growing comfortable with this, the next step is to change the way the stave is viewed. Bring the image to completion and hold it in all its fiery complexity- then proceed to give it dimension. Swing the image about in your vision, see it from under, over, side to side, and finally, place it even with yourself and your vision as though you were standing on a great field with the stave burning on its surface and you observing it from just outside its smoldering form.

From here, choose a BEGINNING POINT, or entry place into the symbol. Once you have done this, give FEEL to the symbol, sensory characteristic in line with the staves meaning and purpose. Color its flames, give them heat or cold, smell and texture. Make it completely real, bringing it out of the imaginary and into the tangible until you are AWARE of it on a level of true completeness. Once this is done, taking care not to rush this most important aspect of the process, bring yourself into it- Enter it- at the point you have chosen. At this time, you should be standing on the stave, with its wholeness laid out in front of you- a Path made of Flame. Your sensory experience as you enter the stave for the first time should be experienced wholly before proceeding. Begin to Walk the path slowly and with conviction, feeling each turn and angle of it, KNOWING its shape, gaining and absorbing its specific might and wisdom into your very core. Often, when traversing a symbol for the first few times, it becomes necessary to bring your vision back above it in the instance that you lose sight of the path while walking it- simply bring it back into view, return to the path at the point you left it, and continue movement. After you have travelled the entirety of the stave and returned back to your starting point of Entry, take a moment or two to truly internalize the experience, then step off the symbol, bring its wholeness back into view, and erase it slowly before coming back into ordinary consciousness.

For those who can master this technique, the creation of galdramyndir specifically for this type of working can be undertaken. Following the Ninefold Way of Knowing in tandem with another's or one's own galdramyndir is an awesome experience of taking in the power of the stave and making it a part of one's Self.

When creating staves for Travel, one can develop further methods, crafting and placing points or centers on the Pathway where he can stop, performing specific ritual or meditation on that point before continuing onward to others along the way in various and increasing levels of complexity and function.

In this fashion the accomplished magician can create entire structures of non-ordinary reality, building them from a galdrastafir foundation within forests of Thought and Ideal- crafting his own Hall of Ritual, each stone, timber, room and window containing special significance and loaded with Intention and Meaning, spending more and more time in meditation, purpose and practice within an architecture of the Will. This method rises from simple beginnings to towering heights of transformative Work.

III. THE LODGE

After having worked with and mastered the Pathways of Fire Discipline, one is prepared to begin the towering feat of The Lodge Discipline. Its application is outlined below, and can be performed continually throughout the rest of the magician's career, ever-changing and being disintegrated and reformed, just as the magician is constantly disintegrating and reforming himself in the process of becoming and self overcoming.

The following Work is intended to be prepared for and utilized as an ongoing process, not necessarily as something to be attempted haphazardly and/or regularly in different manner each time. Rather, the idea is to create for the individual a sacred space that exists outside the realm of corruptibility, completely the magical creation of he who will put the space to use, each twig and timber the decisive construction of specific Intent – each object a Loaded and meaningful piece of Art. A ritual locale intimately known by its creator, unchangeable or usable save by its builder, available at any time for the vitki to bring himself into and Work from. The working builds on the techniques outlined in the Pathways of Fire- it is highly recommended that the vitki has a firm grasp and a great deal of experience with those concepts before attempting this, not because of some imaginary "danger" or other such ridiculousness, but merely from the standpoint of practice and difficulty level.

The previously outlined exercises and ritual are like scale and theory to the musician or lighting and anatomy for the painter: the essential building blocks of more complex compositions. The rules of all forms of Art are similar and infinitely applicable.

Begin by utilizing silence, whether aided or unaided by galdr techniques such as the :I: meditation outlined in Stadhagaldr: A Primer of Physical Runework. It is mandatory to achieve perfect and total stillness before the framework for the following can be structured- any thoughts swirling about must be known and laid to rest, all exterior and interior distractions fed to the Inner Fire. One becomes the Ginnungagap- magically charged emptiness awaiting purpose and form. From here, the vitki opens up the realms of potential and raw material in a controlled and slow fashion- this undertaking Needs to be performed with the awareness heightened and honed; it is important that anything and everything that enters into the equation at this point is deliberately brought there and formed with Intention by the magician himself. Random thought and distraction facilitates the Need to begin again with renewed focus.

Proceed with care and artfulness, shaping the landscape where you will choose to build, from the black earth upward. This part of the working should never be rushed, nor should any part. The entire point is to be familiar with every stone and tree, each droplet of water in the rushing fall, the mountain's heart and the windswept plain. Sink the roots of the trees deep, or grow them from seed to sapling to sighing woods. Lay riverbed with care, and breathe life into the hills- this silent valley is your creation only if you fully know it. Choose your boundary lines and lay them- it is our intention here to create space enough to begin building, not to become sidetracked with other pursuits.

After the landscape is realized, work can begin in earnest on the construction of the ritual chamber itself. The vitki's own creative principles are the only limit here when it comes to architecture: as simple and functional or as complex and beautiful as desired and imagined. My personal recommendation is to start simply under the realization that this sort of construction is limitless in its reception of addition. That is to say, begin building with True Intention and modify, add, or tear down in future visits. Since our desire is to create something we are intimately familiar with, my admonition is to start small, or at least be aware of your mental capacity to remember what you have done each time. Often, a written record can be helpful in solidifying images in the memory- the simple act of writing or drawing one's progress makes another line of connection with his Work.

In this fashion, one might spend his entire first Working constructing a small ritual room, loading each stone with runa, smoothing and reimagining timber and floor until it is just so. He records his progress after the Working, and when he returns, it is exactly as he left it, and he adds furnishing, embellishment, and so on. One might use specific rooms for specific workings, or have a large area set aside within which to perform the Pathways of Fire exercise. The potentials are massive. It cannot be overstressed to take time with each piece of the Working, to turn over each stone of the floor in your hands and know its smoothness or its roughness, its coloring and weight. When you reach for the doorway to enter your Lodge, the feel of the handle should be intimate as a childhood memory. Or, one can artifice this feeling himself, by using bits and pieces of architecture and items from his own deep memories, linking them forever as specific entryways into his own psyche.

Ritual tools can be built and prepared in this place as well, for use during Workings within the Lodgeagain, as long as they are Known on a deep and complete level, there is no limitation save the magicians own.

It is to be understood that the reasons for this working are multi-faceted. Firstly, it has shown itself in personal work to be one of the most difficult and involved techniques for improving the hugauga I have ever undertaken- its benefits on other work that requires the use of the mind's eye (which are myriad!) cannot be overstated. From the basics of rune-meditation, it is quite a long and arduous road to the point where one is working in complexities such as this. Therefore, techniques like this are necessary as challenging innovation and continuation of exercises and principles that dry up or become wearisome and ineffective if not improved upon.

Secondly, it has often shown itself to be the case that one simply cannot always rely on one's own ritual area in the physical realm, whether due to location issues, travel, time constraint or any other reasonwhereas, the accomplished magician has his ritual space always available to him through the use of this technique.

Thirdly, oftentimes ritual areas can be a shared space-residual or lingering presences are not always desirous for those sensitive to such things.

Fourth, it requires not only mental discipline to bring up in detail the created work, but spiritual discipline and Will in order to incorporate it into one's personal regimen often enough to be of use.

Lastly, it familiarizes one on a personal level even more with the principles and concepts of creating Living Work, that is, Workings that can be experienced directly by the spiritual senses and are given a life of their own through the endeavors of the magician, much like taufr on an epic scale. When one thinks of this ritual in terms of taufr-work, its benefits and uses become even more clear. The Lodge is essentially a non-physical taufr- a created object loaded with might and given a doom infinitely more complex than the average talismanic risting.

ᚩ᚛᚜ᚠ

"He listened to his own heart, and heard the sound of his breath rising and falling, and he began to reflect on it. He counted each breath for a day at a time, thinking to himself, "20,000 times I have breathed today. 20,000 shallow breaths, and I have never given mind to it before!" So he gave himself over to the study of his breathing, and lost all count of day or month. Sometimes he would inhale only once an hour, or he would match his exhalations with the falling of a leaf, gaining absolute control of it, and being overwhelmed by a feeling of peace and gratitude each time he was able to draw in air once again. He meditated on the wonderful mysteries of creation, and at the end of one such, he saw in his vision the Great Tree, and heard a sound like the beating of great wings, wings that produced a great wind to rise up and shake the leaves of the Tree, and his heart leaped in his chest as he came back from the sight."

— from *A Crown of Fire.*

The önd is that rushing wind from the beating of the eagle's wings and the breath of fire that quickened the tree on the vast empty shore, giving him life and heat. It's disciplines are to be performed in tandem with those found above: by using them as a starting point for the meditative exercises, the breathing will become regulated, the mind and body cleansed and prepared for further work. However, they are not to be limited to simple meditative prepping- as part of the greater Discipline, one should work toward an ever fuller awareness of his breathing in general, realizing its wondrous dual nature as a gift and giver. The very scientific nature of the breath's transforming one substance and compound to another should be the subject of deep meditation. The following is presented as an addition to those listed in Stadhagaldr I: A Primer of Physical Runework.

ÖND DISCIPLINES

I. THE COSMIC WIND

Like the threefold system of meditative work, this first Discipline is to be performed in successive degree. First, he is to spend at least 30 minutes of time for 3 days simply breathing for an extended period of time. The breath should be deep and even, approximately 10 seconds on inhalation, held for 3 seconds, exhaled for 15 seconds, and held empty for another 2, before beginning the process once more. In this way, one should be breathing only twice a minute, and should work towards the extension of this time until a cycle takes a full minute or more.

Never allow the breathing to become labored or sudden- if this occurs, lessen the amount of time taken in each step.

This part of the Discipline can and should be performed daily, regardless of other work, and can be done as often as one finds himself with spare time to focus on it. Ideally, through the Cosmic Wind Discipline, one will find himself aware of his breathing on a constant level, and will benefit from the regulation thereof.

Second, he is to sit in the traditional meditative pose (demonstrated in the Valknut breathing technique in Stadhagaldr: A Primer of Physical Runework) and visualize the 5 realms of the Central Axis.

He then breathes in through the crown, and down through the successive worlds, vitalizing and becoming fully aware of them as he does so. Upon exhalation, the rushing wind should cleanse and remove all toxic nature from each of them.

Thirdly, he will add to this process the 4 realms of the horizontal axis, allowing the fiery nature of his breath to spiral outward from Midgardhr in his core, permeating and bringing within his consciousness all their form, function and mystery, before proceeding downward from thence.

Through this Discipline, the magician will have spent 9 days on the process of Awakening the Axis, at which point, he should begin the process again with increased difficulty. The desirous result of work with the önd is to become so accustomed to the regulation and rhythmic style of breathing that one is constantly breathing in this fashion without having to dedicate the attention to it.

By continuously working to slow the breathing, one acknowledges that the breath has direct effect on both consciousness and his physical health- the respiratory system supplies all organs and tissues with the necessary vitality to work properly- and that to gain control over it is largely to gain control over himself.

Besides this, the aim is to slow the breathing to a point where the individual can experience those areas of consciousness not normally available to the wakeful human. By placing the bodily rhythm parallel to that of sleep, yet without relinquishing lucid awareness, one becomes able to utilize the roads and rivers between these realms as a wakeful observer rather than a powerless dreamer.

Dissolving the boundaries between what are generally perceived as exclusive areas of consciousness is a great aim of the work at hand, and is difficult and time-consuming. Do not look for overnight success-instead, continue steadily with patience and dedication, and results will follow.

All the exercises in this book should be taken not as something moved through and achieved, but rather as constant exercise to keep the entire Soul Complex conditioned and healthy. Progress should be sought simply through continued application- one should not strive for completion like some sort of athletic competition. When one feels that he has begun to stretch the edges of these disciplines, he should be at a point where new vistas can be created and explored, new boundaries realized and old ones disintegrated-this is the nature of the Work at hand. As soon as a depth is understood or reached, it gives way to further depth and complexity that one could never have realized before reaching his current stage through discipline and rigorous application.

ḢARIR

This reality is a proving ground for magicians. Keep rising. Ever higher. Along pathways of loss, sacrifice, despair, longing and hopelessness, stay unaffected. :W: in all things…traverse the roads of existence impervious to loneliness and despondency, while at that same moment making choices that alienate, separate and sever. Walk among them while being apart from them. Take full part in this consciousness, without being immersed in it to the point of becoming weighed down by it; do this while at that same moment taking full part in heightened consciousness without being destroyed by it. We are unified paradox; we are the face and reverse of the coin, because we see there is only one object, not two. Both face and reverse are the same. Night is a joy after the day, and day is welcomed after the long night, but neither is separate from the other. This would be to say that root and branch are separate from one another because they vary in form and function. Perhaps true in a sense, but both are tree. So, the magician is human, just as he is god. He is individual and he is All. He feels emotion, but is unaffected. He experiences this life, but is not attached to it. He is carnal and abstinent, cruelty and mercy.

I begin by saying that being hamramr, shape-strong, is a fetterless existence of being unattached to any one particular seeming or being- we all must choose our hamr each day, each moment, and drape it over the soul. The practice of shape-shift leads the thoughtful magician inevitably to the question: who am I really? The answer to this question usually lies somewhere entangled in the shadowy realms between choice, experience and conditioning. If it is our goal to live our lives Initiated and reborn into an unconditioned mode of living, hamramr offers us a new way of looking at ourselves and our interactions with the world around us.

Hamr, heiti and hamingja are inextricably linked ideas that form a complex hierarchy of power and transformative energy within the soul structure and skill-set of the accomplished magician. By hamr, we are referring to That Which is Presented- the seeming of the individual, if you will; the driving persona that the magician has chosen to meet the world about him face to face with. By hamingja, we are referring to that accumulated might and personal power and luck that the individual has gained through reaping the Works he has sown- all effective magical work, hamramr included, relies on hamingja to drive it; for this reason, it is all-important that the dedicated magician continuously perform Great Works, thereby being led to another. By heiti, we are referring to those Names that the magician has chosen for his various shapes and seemings, giving them more concrete reality and grounding by assigning them a vibration. Not all hamr must have heiti, however, and generally only very strong and defined hamr are given names, making them easier to assume and giving them their own Wyrd and function.

The forms that hamr can take are limitless- however, it becomes easy to think in terms of might and majesty and overlook the subtle, practical applications that can become a powerful tool in the hands of one well versed in their usage. The freedom that hamr-shift affords its cunning user opens a world of possibilities, because it allows the magician to meet any situation, no matter how diverse, with its perfect match. The sniveling weakling slinks away from a challenging scenario, bemoaning his lot in life: "if only I was more like this or that. If only I was able to act or react in such and such a fashion." The magician holds on to no such feeble excuses. He simply shifts his hamr accordingly and meets the issue head on with ferocity, cunning, deceptiveness, honor, strength, kindness, cruelty, or whatever is called for. He is able to do this, because as a shape-strong individual, he has broken the fetters and boundaries of self containment and realized that he can be whatever he needs to be- he has no limitation or set parameter of being. He assumes the form that is needed, day by day, moment by moment.

That archetype of the northern magician has been called Svipall among his many other heiti. Svipall translates as "the ever changing." He is the god of fetter-destruction, of masking, of wandering and being unknown in each place until such a time as he chooses to reveal himself in the hamr and heiti by which he is recognized. By separating ourselves from the worn out idea that we are bound by our own persona, we can come to the realization that we are every persona- we only need slip the mask on and become it for as long as we choose, shattering the single strand of our Wyrd into myriad threads, weaving and twisting and spiraling their way to a greater destiny.

The only danger in this Work is forgetfulness. We can sometimes slip into a hamr so fully, so completely immersed, that we forget the fluid nature of this existence, and we allow the chains of circumstance and self deception to encircle our limbs. We say to ourselves those words of power: I Am This. And by the saying, we become it, and must struggle once again to rediscover the truth of freedom and the song of fetter-bursting.

The Disciplines required to work with one´s Hamr are varied and difficult in explanation, due to the formless and fluid nature of the subject at hand, and because of this, must be worked at diligently and with a deep application of the other areas of the soul complex.

HAMR DISCIPLINES

I. THE SACRED ENCLOSURE

The Discipline of Hamramr is three-fold, like the others above. Beginning with a simply chosen object, of inanimate nature (i.e. a rock, stick, etc.), the magician places it on the ground in front of him, and makes a circular mark round about it. It is best to begin with an object of natural origin rather than artificial, although these can be used later on as the individual becomes more familiar with the exercise. The circle is drawn to focus the intention and attention, as well as to represent the Sacred Enclosure from which this Discipline draws its name. Centering all the focus one can muster, he begins breaking the object down to its basest components and ideas. What does it physically consist of? What is its function? What is its nature? Where did it come from, and what will become of it? What does it feel and smell and taste like? What is the difference between its outer and inner texture and makeup? As these questions are answered, the magician starts to bring himself in line with those answers.

He shuts off his own pre-conceptions of self awareness, and instead, he creates a new form, function and being independent of those ideas. In essence, he splits off of himself, and recreates an entirely new self in tandem with the truths answered about this object in the circle, placing himself within that sacred space in order to fully become the object of his study. As stated before, this is a very difficult and demanding endeavor, and cannot be fully mastered by irregular or distracted application.

The second part uses a more abstract idea, and incorporates the elements referred to throughout the Germanic cosmogony myth- the discovery of these Elements, and the study of them is a worthy pursuit on its own – for 9 days, the magician uses the above technique, but instead of performing it with a simple object, he uses one element at a time, focusing not just on their physical makeup, but the greater ideas and mythological implications of their use in the Cosmogony.

Thirdly, he observes a living thing and uses it as the focus of his Discipline. This final part of the process is by far the most involved, due to the complexity of the subject. (Let the magician not forget that all of the previous parts of this process have been with single objects, fragments of the cosmos, but that each living, animated thing is representative of the whole.) Upon the deeper mastery of this Discipline and the principles and secrets it holds for the dedicated, a myriad of uses begin to unfold- studying and discovering these uses and applications is the second and hidden part of the Discipline of Hamramr.

HAMINGJA

As everything in this cosmic dream is linked together, so too, each part of the soul complex cannot be taken entirely as individual, save to make clarification and educate us while we remain aware that these separations are not truly there. Because of this, ideas like Will and Hamingja must flow together, just as the Hugr and Minni are not really separate concepts, but sides of the same coin. Therefore, we cannot limit our scope of these things to the mundane or microscopic without looking at the awesome, macrocosmic nature of them as well. In this way, our understanding of the whole mosaic must broaden before it can hone in on the tiny piece of glass that forms only the center of the pupil in a great scene that contains within it many eyes, many faces and many forms.

When we speak of the hamingja, we are generally referring to an individual's personal power and Will that fluctuates by his own actions and Wyrd, and that of those he is bound to, whether by blood, oath, or circumstance. This explanation quickly shows how massive and complex of an idea hamingja is- it cannot be taken simply as "Will" or "spiritual might," because the reality outshines that idea as the sun outshines a candle. The hamingja can, indeed, be seen as the essence and vitality of the soul complex, and its elevation and sustaining are essential in order to elevate and sustain all other areas- in this way, hamingja is like the Ouroboros, or the Jormungandr, the serpent swallowing itself. It must be fed, in order to feed.

What it feeds on are actions and words that lead the individual from one great word and deed to another, and as the hamingja is raised, it invigorates and empowers the soul to perform greater and greater acts. Its building and sustaining is much like a fire – at first, small and uncertain, putting off smoke and choking at the tiniest challenge to its flickering flame, fed slowly at first with small and modest offerings, until it can handle the burning of greater fuels.

In a short amount of time, anything can be fed into its roaring maw and as long as there is fuel continuously fed to it, it will grow ever greater and greater, even beating back the darkness of night, and attracting everything to itself with its majestic beauty. In our lives, we must constantly find fuel to feed this fire. In our practice, this fuel is called ritual. To further understand the idea of ritual and the sacred creation of the cosmos, and its connection to Will and hamingja, we must understand the concept of Galdr.

At the very depths of the human condition there lies a great calm and a great answer. Out of the void and Abyss, a light shines constant: that gem in the blackness is Will. From the madness, the crawling, the blindness, we may ascend on those glorious golden wings, if we but Will it. No man can touch that true source until he has dwelt in the darkness of Suffering and :N:eed- it is these things that spur the traveler onward, out of despondency and self-doubt, if he does not first succumb to them in weakness.

Like a jewel hanging alone in the endless firmament, our destiny and desire burn without flickering; it is only we who falter. Any action not toward that flame is betrayal. A traitorous action of the highest caliber, for the treason is committed against our very Being, our place in the cosmos for good or ill. If we allow the poisoned blade of Hopelessness and Heartlessness to strike against our destiny, unrealized as yet, we have truly lost the battle of Ascendancy. The enemy is our own Fear and Doubt- and they are merciless foes, ever advancing in ruthless formation.

But our weapon is this Will – it strikes and parries with grace and poise and brutal efficiency. We have only to grasp it and bring it to bear in our lives, so that even at the lowest of lows we may hold our heads high and proclaim: "This will fade away. For this is not my Will, and therefore shall become dust and be cast aside like ash on the wind. I am like the highest star in the heavens, and this is but a shimmer in my constant light. I will rise above this as a king of the forest above the saplings."

Galdr is the manifestation of this Will on the physical plane. It manifests itself as sound, from a tiny whisper to a great roaring, it is the directed force given vibratory quality. Every galdr sung is a reordering of the entire cosmos, a shifting of that great Universal Thought; we remake the world in each syllable. The sound rises up from the deepest core of our being and goes forth into the farthest reaches of Existence- erasing the distinction between ourselves and that which seems to be apart from us.

The form of Man is the form of the cosmos- from dust to star, everything is in him, and he in everything. God, Universe, Planet, Man, Woman, Beast, Plant, Stone. All words indicate a separation that does not truly exist- all is connection, all is Self. The Will of One is the Will of the All-thing.

As the sound issues forth, laden with intention and pure focus, it simply becomes so. When we give sound to an idea, we give it form and substance immediately. "I am hungry," we say, and we can think of nothing but our hunger, for we have claimed it to be what we are. "I am weak," we say, and weakness permeates every strand of our essence.

From the beginning of matter, a meeting of Fire and Ice- This fated union produces the Roarer, pure sound and might, a mass of pure potential, given ultimate form by the three brothers: Inspiration, Will and Holiness. The First Galdr brings forth the pattern for all others.

We tap into that roaring might within ourselves, that raw place that exists within us, a chaotic world of swirling potential, where everything exists as a possibility simply waiting to be NAMED, to be given a life, to be brought from chaos and uncertainty into a more tangible form of being. Through our Inspiration, we grasp it, and craft its purpose and function, its sound, its nature. Through our Will, we forge it from its base materials, bringing beauty and art to shapelessness. Through our holiness, we make it sacred and whole, a living thing imparted with Self, just as all things in this Existence are Self, and are filled with the same. Through this primal process, we have given life to a whisper of thought. We have transformed ourselves, by which we have transformed the cosmos, for these words are one and the same.

Our songs come from Within. The development and refining of these songs is a long process that happens naturally over time as we use them, alter them, reshape and sing them through the Worlds. They are flowing things, not tied down by definite form or rule, moving from us to wend their way- we are a generative point for something that, once realized, becomes greater than us. Their purpose and effects are manifold, and range from simple evocations of joy and love of life, to complex formulae designed to be sung by many people for mighty change. More so, as our hamingja grows, so does our realization: each word becomes a galdr, sending ripples through the Well and running through the Great Tree from root to leaf. Our Intention becomes everything and has potential to preserve or to poison. Our words can be kindness or curse, honeyed or hateful- and from Understanding the power of these things, we learn to control them and ourselves. Nobility and high-mindedness can now be seen as all encompassing and of great importance, as we begin to grasp our responsibility for each word as it spirals outward and away from us, an incantation for good or ill.

We are born into this world completely involved in self and blind to the Self. Covered in darkness, devoid of Love, we exist as a manifestation of Will without Wholeness- desperate and grasping, like an infant that wants but does not reason, it consumes but does not question, it screams and thrashes and strives only for its immediate desire.

Transforming, from a glimmer in shadow, we begin to Know Ourselves as Indivisible and immortal; the seed at the center of Cosmos. Worlds without pale to those Within as we explore the hundred realms of Self, rising and falling along the Central Axis as our understanding grows of :T: After we grasp its mysteries for ourselves through Ordeal on the Tree, the Halls of Hel and death hold no more terror for those who have dwelt at the silent depths.

Truth is a lonely traveler; we are now set to forever sojourn in the lands of Emptiness and Sacrifice. From deep inside the Self, the universe unfolds- manifest and unmanifest at once, its supreme laws laid down only to be broken free of, to put that giant to death and build our own world from his body . From those bones we shape ourselves; from that corpse, the flower of becoming grows. In this blood, we wash clean of the transient, unite with the principles of living and dying, free from the shackles of both joy and sorrow. Seated on the throne of the eternal and unchanging, we rise and outshine the sun with the glory of continuous light from the Heart of Understanding.

The Disciplines included here are by no means exhaustive, and are meant as a supplement to those performed within your Greater Work. They can be looked at as instructive, or simply to inspire daily ritual of your own creation. The important part of this is to always remember that ritual should be fuel to feed the hamingja, and the hamingja should be the fuel that feeds your ritual. There is a rune embedded deeply into this circular principle.

To consecrate ourselves to a concept daily through simple word is a powerful tool of hamingja development. These daily prayers are not to a god, save that which is Within. It is to continually state and form our intention to change ourselves, to forge ourselves in the way which we have chosen through this regular SPEAKING or NAMING of our becoming Wyrd, we place the power of transformation firmly in our own hands.

HAMINGJA DISCIPLINES

CENTRAL AXIS CONSECRATION

:U: Galdr

From the depths, I have centered myself- the voices of my ancestors speak through me. My might is quiet and calm, for I have realized that in silence there is strength; in stillness there is a great power.

:A: Galdr

To the heights I have raised myself- I have realized my Divinity and my spiritual growth is constant- I sacrifice my self to my Self. If I am to Keep Rising I must help others to rise as well. My soul streams ever sunward.

:I: Galdr

I am my own creation. If I wish to change myself, I need only enact the change through hard work and discipline. I drive out the bad iron in the fires of ordeal, and forge myself stronger each day.

:E: Galdr

I am master of my mind and body. By keeping them whole and healthy, my entire Being is elevated. I am a slave until I learn to be lord of my own life; therefore, I will strive daily to control and eliminate that which is base and impure.

:O: Galdr

I am All. By mastering that which is within, I am master of that which is without. I will continue to build Love, Patience, Will and Understanding by constant dedication to that which is Eternal and Unchanging.

***

NASU RITE

Begin by facing each cardinal direction and intoning the compass point in Old Norse. (Nordhri, Austri, Sudhri, Vestri.) The initial sound for each of these will make up the body of the following rune galdr, using the staves :N: :A: :S: :U:

The purpose of this rite is to provide a sense of centeredness and connection in the magician, emphasized by the count of the formula :A: and the tally :H:. The compass points imply the whole of creation, everything in all directions, the primal seed :H: created and made manifest by Divine Will :A:.

The galdr should be performed with an easy rise and fall in intonation, first singing each entire rune name (for which I use the monosyllabic Younger runes) individually nine times on three breaths. (Naudh, naudh, naudh *breathe*) Then, intone the formula slowly, on a one to one breath ratio, nine more times. After this initial preparation, the formula can begun to be sung in a circular fashion, that is, constantly and without break until breathing deeply and continuing.

One will discover the Hidden Word within the galdr after a short time of cyclical singing, that being SUNA, the sun that our solar system revolves round. As the Hidden Word comes to the surface of the galdr, the vitki can begin singing the formula :SOL::SUNA::SIGUR::SOWILO: creating a 3-4-5-6 rune count.

The might of creation and transformation :3/TH: combined with Divine Will :4/A: and Right Action :5/R: sets one on the path toward Illumination :6/K:

Adding the numbers of each count together brings us to 18 :B: (which combines down to 9, :H:) and includes the mysteries of cycling existence, Being, Becoming, Fading Away. A look into the individual tallies shows an even further connection with the runes :C::R::TH:

After time spent with the Hidden Words, one returns back to the NASU galdr, and then back to the single rune forms, and to silence.

MINNI

The memory center of the Soul Complex, working in close alignment with the Hugr, or cognitive process the instant after something is perceived, it is placed into the great storehouse of the Minni, where it can be called forth and utilized over and over. There are good reasons why these two areas are presented as twin ravens on each shoulder of the Lord of Knowledge- where one fails, the other is not much good.

Both can be sharpened and exercised, flying out on their black wings and returning to land on the magician's shoulders with diverse wisdom.

MINNI DISCIPLINES

The Disciplines of the Minni are perhaps more straightforward than some of the others, but no less important, nor less difficult in their own right.

I. VEGVISIR

The first is the Vegvisir Discipline. In order to be master over his own experiences, one must be able to recall where he has been, and what he has done. Beginning with a day at a time, close the eyes in meditation and do away with all distraction. When this has been completed to satisfaction, the magician will retrace every event of the day, starting with just before he closed his eyes and began the discipline.

It is quickly discovered that even in the same day as the technique takes place, this endeavor can be very elusive- with continued practice and application, successful navigation of one's own immediate past can turn up a great deal of otherwise missed insights. As skill grows in this area, the magician should increase the amount of time between the discipline and its remembered day, using the days in between as a bridge to aid the memory if necessary.

II. STOREHOUSE OF WISDOM

Secondly, the magician will work with memorization, which differs greatly from the first Discipline instead of simply recalling past events, he will be deliberately entering information into his Minni until it remains there to be utilized. Like any store-room, items left inside and never used or upkept will moulder and rot, becoming completely unrecognizable and worthless; likewise, the storage space is finite and should not be cluttered and stuffed with useless items- it requires maintenance and frequent cleaning and organizational processes. The Disciplines of Minni are just such a process- they keep the passageways well trod, and place precedence on putting things of value inside.

In utilizing the Storehouse of Wisdom Discipline, it is strongly recommended that the magician choose a passage of value to him at least once monthly and undergo a rigorous memorization technique to ensure it is not held with a tenuous grasp- over time, and with the continued recitation of what he has accumulated, the individual will truly be a Storehouse of the Wisdom of the ages. Discretion must be used, therefore, to make certain that the quality of what he retains is high.

III. THE BRIDLED TONGUE

The third discipline is that of the Bridled Tongue, which is two-fold. On the one hand, the magician will gain mastery over his own speech, and on the other, he will broaden the scope of that speech. First, each week, he will choose one word in his vocabulary to maintain a bridle over. Each time he uses this word, he will make a mark of it. This can be done in the old-fashioned way as a cut to the flesh, or, for the more gentle, a simple tally can be kept in a pocket book or other such record. At the end of each day, the tally can be used as a debt to be worked off in some way in order to make the individual less hasty with his speech the following day. For example, for each mark, the magician could perform a either a physical exercise or austerity such as jogging a mile or holding a difficult staða for a set amount of time. The idea is to make the penalty severe enough that even if it is physically or mentally beneficial, it is still useful in aiding the control of the speech.

The second portion of this discipline is for the magician to begin the study of language. Initially, this can be the further development or comprehension of his own native tongue, but should quickly move on to the study and application of at least one other. This can then be used in tandem with the Storehouse Discipline, as his memorization increases to texts in their original languages.

It should come as no surprise that those who were considered wise in many cultures thought the study of language to be one of the principal ways to increase knowledge and understanding- even those who have only entered into a cursory study of the Runes are utilizing this discipline. By acknowledging that words and their vibratory quality have power over the world around us, we acknowledge that thorough study and understanding of the principles behind this idea are worthwhile, and necessary for one to become a man of wisdom.

LÍK

The lík is the Hall of the Blood, the Chariot of the
Soul, and the Holy Temple of the Inner Fire. It is the
microcosmic representative of Yggdrasil, the great
World Tree, and as the rune poem says: Yew Holds
All.

All parts of the soul are dependent on the others, and
as such, the body is a sacred thing. This being the
case, it must be treated accordingly- we must look to
not only beautify it, but to keep it cleansed and whole.
Even if we pollute it deliberately, we must find the
balance by then purifying and renewing; if we allow
it to remain polluted and filled with detritus, that
pollution and detritus will begin to corrupt and
unbalance us. With no care or control of the Lík, we
can never move our focus to the other realms of the
soul, as its weaknesses and unhealthiness will distract

our consciousness and leave it trapped in the cares and concerns of our physical well-being.

If it is truly the representative of the entire cosmos, then it must be healthy, strong, beautiful and functioning at its highest level. For within us run the roads and rivers between the worlds, Sól and Máni, and all the holy places of our continuing existence- we must not neglect this duty to keep our bodies an outward manifestation of our inward strength and purity.

Again, as we begin to understand the interconnectedness of the Soul Complex, we see that through correctly applied work in one area, the desire to improve and strengthen another naturally arises. This is equally true of work with the lík- its exercises and disciplines lead to a feeling of cleansed well being that lends itself perfectly to continuous beneficial work in other areas, and transforms our body into a work of Art, a finely fashioned vehicle to bear the Fire.

By simply taking a non-violent approach to our dealings with our own bodies, we set the groundwork for a healthy relationship with it. "Doing no harm" to the lík should include, in addition to the disciplines listed here, watching one's diet, not allowing a sedentary lifestyle to waste the physical carriage, and not subjecting it to the punishment and poisoning of excessive substance intake such as drugs or alcohol.

Abstinence and moderation are the by-words of disciplining the lík- this is because most problems that arise within the lík are the result of negative choices made by the individual regarding what he introduces into it. We must exercise caution and control with those things we desire that are unhealthy for us. The idea of mastering our desires is a large part of the Work we have dedicated ourselves to- it is not fitting that this principle fail to make its presence known in this area of the Soul Complex as well.

Continued improvement and care over the lík is a must. If we grow complacent, slack in our practice, lazy and over-indulged, then we become weak. Our hamingja plummets, and leaves us scattered, confused, and at the mercy of reaction. On the other hand, fulfilling our discipline in this area brings focus, an energized mental capacity, and an obvious benefit to our physical appearance and well-being.

LÍK DISCIPLINES

I. STAÐAGALDR

The magician should begin, if he has not already, a daily staðagaldr routine, preferably in the morning shortly after rising. The techniques and meditations that accompany this are outlined in SG. If desired, other traditional methods of physical control can and should be utilized.

II. DRINK THY MEASURE

The magician should choose each week, one thing to abstain from, whether that be alcohol, a certain type or ingredient of food, sexual activity, or some recreational act that is potentially harmful or numbing to the mind. The aim of this discipline is to give the magician a fuller mastery over his desires in this way, he chooses for himself what he will do, rather than giving in to compulsory activities, or falling into negative routines. At any time the individual feels himself giving in to compulsion rather than deliberately chosen action, he must immediately give that thing up for a period of time to rebalance and regain control of himself. This takes an immense self-inspection and honesty to be aware of- here there is no room for the self deceiver, or one who wallows in self pity or weakness- we seek to become masters of our own lives and souls; one who acts from compulsion will be a slave until he destroys that compulsion by understanding its root and removing it.

III. THE CHIEFTAIN'S SON

The connection between asceticism, spiritual liberation and the martial cult is one of extreme importance in both the Germanic and the Indo-Aryan traditions. From the young men in the warrior cults of Germany and Scandinavia who took Odin as their patron and performed esoteric ritual and spiritual practices as part of their martial way of life, to the Vratyas and Keshins of north-east India, we see the symbolic interconnectedness of the nature of spiritual and physical warfare. Living on the edge of accepted society, the one who renounces traditional life within the normal social confines has chosen a mode of being that defies norms and requires a complete dedication to self-perfection on all levels.

For this reason, the accomplished magician should undertake a martial skill and apply his understanding of it and the learning thereof into his spiritual life. Each individual on this path should be powerful and capable in all areas of life- here, the importance is on the thought process, the extreme self-discipline required and the awareness and confidence that one gains through practice and study of the martial arts, not to mention the increased abilities of flexibility, physical strength and fortitude and so on.

It is presumed that the individual has already developed for themselves a healthy diet and regular exercise regimen in addition to these added disciplines. Diet and exercise are obviously keys to living a balanced and strong lifestyle- there is no replacement for these two things. The disciplines and practices of the lik are manifold, and dealt with in a deeper fashion on other works by this author.

ÓÐR

Ecstasy.   Madness.   Inspiration.   Elevated consciousness. All are words that can be used to describe óðr, but all fall short in their limited scope. Rather than something that overcomes and possesses, it is something to be attained, a thing to gain mastery over and to call upon at will.

In most texts, this area of the Soul Complex is explained in a much simplified fashion as that feeling that one is overcome by during war, sexual activity, or in the deepest throes of poetic inspiration. While these may not be inaccurate, it is also of a shallow nature compared to what can be gained from further study of the myth surrounding it, and applying that concept within the framework of our ongoing quest for self-overcoming.

We must look deeply into the myth of Óðinn's quest for Óðroerir, or the Stirrer of Inspiration, to find many symbolic meanings that will aid us in our understanding of the Óðr.

After first realizing his goal, and learning its location through a series of events, he approaches the mountainside where his prize is hidden; an inert, cold dwelling place, wherein resides Gunnloð, the sleeping maiden, guardian over the three vats that hold the wondrous nectar. Óðinn transforms himself into a serpent in order to make his way into the chamber that holds the mead of inspiration, and once inside, he sleeps with the maiden for three consecutive nights so that he might take in the liquid and return with it to Asgarðr.

Here in this simple story, a great mystery is revealed: within the depths of ourselves lies this powerful energy, awaiting an activator to make use of it. By traversing the pathways into that hidden area of ourselves, the belly of the earth, deep in the core, we come to this place where our goal lies. The maiden guarding the nectar is seduced and the resulting heat generated from this union of opposites leads to the unlocking or activating of this energy. It is consumed in three measures, upon which time it is raised from the depths unto the heights, showering all around it with its wondrous might.

Rigorous meditation on this idea is required in order to understand one of the most hidden secrets implied in the Edda, awaiting the one who possesses the strength to attain it.

ÓÐR DISCIPLINES

The exercises surrounding the awakening of this fiery energy that elevates the consciousness and brings vitality and regeneration to the entirety of the Soul Complex are deliberately varied. There are many ways to achieve this awakening, and experiementation in this process is encouraged, albeit with an organized and intention-based method. This area of practice is likely to see the most failure and need for extreme concentration, which must be gained by a firm grasp on the meditation principles and disciplines set forth in the Hugr section of this work.

I. AWAKENING THE MAIDEN

For the first discipline, it is helpful to look first at the myth of Kvasir, who was formed from the energy and essence of all the gods and goddesses, by reconciling and mingling their life-force, and who represented that fiery nature that was at their core- he was then murdered and his blood transmuted into the Mead of Inspiration. In this discipline, the magician seeks to awaken that fire in his core, to generate that heat and vitality of essence that was present in Kvasir's Blood.

The magician begins by attaining concentration and rhythm of breath as laid out in the Hugr and Önd sections. He then turns his entire concentration to the area of Svartalfheim between the navel and the groin region, and focuses on awakening the energy lying dormant there. Using the myth of the mountain cavern as his basis of concentration, the magician bores a hole through the stone walls and transforms himself in order to go inside that area in which lies the sleeping maiden. He then begins to generate friction and heat within the cavern, so as to gain access to those vessels in which the nectar is held. At this point, the desired effect is to begin awakening a great heat in the core, that fiery generation that comes from "awakening the maiden." This must be done through trial and error, and one should not become sidetracked with other events that may occur during this process – nor should he be taken in by imaginary results.

II. THE VESSELS

Boðn, Són, Óðroerir. The names themselves, although perhaps not predating Snorri's Edda, can be used as focus points as well: Boðn, or "vessel." Són, or "reconciliation." And finally, Óðroerir, "the stirrer or activator of Óðr." After Awakening the Maiden, one has crossed the threshold of the endeavor, and approaches the next stage. Boðn is one vessel, like the magician- solitary, representing an inside and an outside, a single entity. Són, on the other hand, is the reconciliation of the one with its other- the unification of opposites that is necessary to reach the third and final vessel which holds the sought after content of this discipline. At this point, the magician consumes these principles and energies within himself in three measured draughts, emptying them into himself completely, filling his being with their essence and heat that has been generated prior to this stage. He is then ready to proceed.

III. THE CROWN OF FIRE

Now, transforming himself once again, the magician brings the Óðr upwards, towards the crown represented in the realm of Asgardhr. This stage is the culmination of the work- the fire of óðr burns all in its path on its journey up through the hvels, before returning once again to its place in the depths. Raising the óðr into the heights is to set on one's head the Crown of Fire, and to be permeated by that nectar in one's entirety. But often, on the journey upward, the Óðr is lost, scattered amongst the lower realms and drips slowly back to the depths of being, where it must be sought after again and again until it reaches its place in the highest seat.

The Disciplines of Óðr are lifelong endeavors, and mastery over them comes through mastery of all the realms of Self.

FYLGJA

Work with the fylgja has always been stunted in the past by preconception. We have been told what it is, what to expect, its purpose and function, how it will "appear" to us, that it is something that "appears" to us at all- all of these notions are things that have been taken for granted and have potentially harmed or limited our ability to see new growth in this area.

Instead of discussing what the fylgja is, attempting to fence it in with vague notions of "protective force" or "astral body," we shall instead dispel these limiting factors and begin afresh with our work in developing this area of the Complex.

Much like weight training, it is difficult for the individual to properly exercise a specific muscle group until one is able to feel that muscle working- we must use this analogy as we approach the lesser-known and understood areas of our own Self- through trial and error, if need be, we shall begin to feel out these unmapped territories and from there, seek to develop them.

For now, instead of concerning oneself with concrete ideas of what the fylgja "is" as an unchanging constant, let us think instead about it in potential- what it can be. Through all the things we have explored within this work, the areas of the Soul Complex, we seem to be lacking that difficult to describe or pinpoint aspect of the self that would fill the realm of the intuition, the instinct, the "imagination"- that is, if the Hugr creates The Lodge, is it the fylgja that visits it? If the hamingja is built up as a fire that can be felt and transferred, is it the fylgja that senses it? The word itself, "fetch" is somewhat telling here, but personal work and experimentation must occur in order to bring this out of the area of speculation.

Because the nature of this work will begin as largely uncharted territory for each magician, our disciplines within this realm of the Soul Complex must remain fluid as well as rigorous and documented. The biggest danger in this sort of practice is falling victim to or own desires and allowing ourselves to be fooled by what we wish to see instead of what is actually there; this pitfall is the most common to snare the magician in nearly every aspect of his Work, and has taken in many.

Work should be undertaken in a very ordered fashion and documented closely, with result (or lack thereof) being carefully studied and analyzed. Changes should be made in the practice in an organic and natural fashion, as needed, but not until one technique or approach has been exhausted and proven either effective or ineffective for the individual. This is also a difficult subject to ascertain with certainty it is expected (or hoped) that through development and disciplined work in other areas that the magician has by now grown exponentially in his work and built up a solid foundation on which to proceed. For this reason, work with the fylgja is best experimented with in a more full fashion after the individual has mastered or deeply engaged in the other disciplnes and has through them, and his other constant disciplne attained the level of Journeyman.

FYLGJA DISCIPLINES

Rather than a set of disciplines pertaining to it, work with the fylgja must come from a more organic root, and the application thereof will reflect this.

Beginning exercises with the fetch should be a simple process of attempted awareness. As discussed previously, we cannot work with a thing we cannot feel- in order for this awareness to take place, deep meditation must occur to find this area of the complex and to slowly define its borders (and lack thereof). Attention should be given to the Old Norse (one possible being "that which accompanies") translations of this word, and its connection to the hamingja, the family line, the sleeping consciousness and its potential nature. This should be an intensely personal focus, and I cannot recommend its open discussion with anyone at this point of the process- the very idea of the fylgja is one that can only grow and develop within your own Self- outside suggestion and conception are likely to do more harm than good at this stage of your practice. After discovery and Knowing this area, the individual's Work and practice with it will undoubtedly proceed in the proper direction.

The author would only make the following :N:eedful closing statements: Re-explore the entire Soul Complex in an attempt to find those pieces that seem to be "missing" or "unbalanced." Through honest effort and self examination, the Work at hand will open itself and continually deepen to those who seek "those roots which no man Knows."

Ask yourself questions about your spiritual practice, whether or not your notions of certain concepts truly come from Within, or whether they have been totally shaped by outside influence. Obviously, when we begin our Work, a great deal of what we do will be heavily influenced by outside sources (such as the book you hold now), but it becomes more and more necessary and desirable as you proceed along the Roads and Rivers of the Nine Worlds that you tear down your methods and re-experience them without conditioning.

Is your approach intellectual or experiential? That is, can you honestly say that your Work is developing through direct experience, or have you rationalized and reduced your Work into clever statements, posturing and self-deluding aggrandizement?

Is your work growing in an organic fashion that displays itself in your life without the need for boastful action or word? Or have you succumbed to the "group display" that so often plagues those on this road?

Knowing the Self and finding balance are spiritual endeavors that have spurred on countless brave and high-minded individuals through the ages. This booklet is in no way intended to act as a "be all and end all" solution, nor even a solution at all. Like any writing, it is simply the opinion and experience of an individual, shared with the hope that it might aid other individuals in achieving a life of Inspired Action.

I sincerely hope that you found this humble text of some value in that goal.

Paul Waggener, Yule 2011

Part II
A Crown Of Fire

A young man seeking to understand the mysteries of the universe and to become a man of knowledge and power decided one day to seek out those that were reported to have the answers to his questions. First, his footsteps led him to the temple in the center of the town, its pillars and gilded roof shining brightly in the sun. He walked up the great wide stairs that led within, past marble fountains and robed temple maidens, priests at their prayers in vast vaulted rooms with images of the gods carved into stone. He came to the chambers of the high priest, and approached the high, gem studded chair upon which he sat. "I am a young man seeking direction from one who understands the Hidden Mysteries," he said, inclining his head respectfully to the high priest, resplendent in his fine robes and the chains of his station. "What must I do to become a man of knowledge, to explore the depths of man's nature and understand the secrets of the universe?"

The priest considered the young man with the look of one who is full of love for all creatures high and low, his face gentle and noble and fatherly, and answered him, "In order to become a man of knowledge, and to explore the depths of man's nature and understand the secrets of the universe, you must know God."

"And how am I to know God?"

"To know God you must read the scriptures and the sacred texts, you must observe the rituals of the faith, and you must control your base nature through prayer and fasting."

"These things I will do," said the young man, earnestly in search of the Truth. From that day forward, he pored over the scriptures and all the holy texts, he observed with unshakable dedication the rituals and days of observance, performed all the proper sacrifices and prayed and fasted constantly. At the end of three years, he sought out the priest again. "I have done all that you have asked of me, with full dedication and applied myself ceaselessly to the precepts laid out in the scripture."

"You have done this with great diligence and humility," said the priest. "And what have you learned?"

"By reading the scriptures and sacred texts, I have learned that words by themselves are meaningless. By observing the rituals and making sacrifices, I have learned that ritual is empty when performed for its own sake. By praying, I have learned that talking to an empty room is useless without intention. By fasting I have learned that hunger and thirst are nothing to a man who can eat and drink and still feel a hunger and thirst unquenched by ceremony and spectacle."

The priest smiled at his answers with patience and understanding. "Perhaps this then, is not the place for you yet," he said. "But if you should ever choose to return, we would welcome you back with open arms."

The young man turned his footsteps towards a certain house he knew, where a man reputed to be a great alchemist lived. Upon knocking, the door was answered by the alchemist's servant, who showed him in.

"What is it that you are here for?" asked the alchemist, stroking his luxuriant beard.

"I am here to understand the mysteries of the cosmos and know the great hidden truths of this existence," said the young man. "I have already looked for them in the temple, and have not found what I was seeking."

The alchemist laughed heartily. "No, you will not find the truth in a temple. I will take you as my apprentice, and show you how to make wondrous mixtures and solutions, produce gold from base metals, and coax fire out of stone."

"What must I do to learn these things?" The young man asked.

"You must study the ancient treatises on alchemy, and learn diverse tongues in order to read the more difficult texts. You must plumb the depths of complex formulas in order to understand the composition of the very substances that make up the universe, and you must ceaselessly and tirelessly apply these ideas in order to create the Elixir of Life and the Philosopher's Stone."

"I will do these things," the young man agreed.

For the three years that followed, the young man spent every waking hour turning the pages of massive codexes and treatises on the subject of alchemical study, puzzling over and gaining the mastery of many languages in this way. He learned countless secret formulas, initiating himself into the secret methods of the process of creating First Matter, that stuff from which the very stars are formed. Finally, he achieved the creation of the Stone, turning base metals like lead into great quantities of gold and growing rich in the so doing. The Elixir of Life became known to him, and he drank from its nectar.

At the end of the third year, he approached the venerable alchemist, saying, "I have applied myself thoroughly to the principles you have taught me, and studied them tirelessly for the count of three years."

"You have indeed, my young friend, and in doing so, have surpassed even me in such a short time. What have you learned from your time here?"

The young man thought for a moment, before speaking. "In studying the ancient treatises I have learned that the largest of books sometimes contain the smallest amounts of wisdom. Through the studying of diverse languages, I have learned that expression is limited and restrictive in any tongue or all of them at once, and that none of them are sufficient to contain the Great Mysteries. In studying and mastering the secret formulas I have learned that physical matter is transitory and largely meaningless. In the creation of the Philosopher's Stone, I have learned that only by beginning with gold can someone create more of it- that is to say, the gold is there all along, only waiting to be uncovered and multiplied. And in the creation of the Elixir of Life, I have learned immortality is not agelessness, it is merely the freedom from the fear of death and the fetters of life.

The alchemist smiled, and nodded slowly. "You have learned many things, but I can see you have not found what you are seeking. Go on your way with my friendship."

So the young man left the great house of the alchemist and went on his way to the forest beyond town, and approached the hut of a magician that was rumored to live there. On the third day of seeking, he found the small thatched hut, where human skulls adorned the doorway and strange symbols and markings snaked along the lintel. Before he could knock, the door opened and the magician greeted him.

"I know what you seek. Begone from here unless you are prepared to make the necessary sacrifices." The magician was strange to behold, both terrible and beautiful at the same time, the ashes on his face and arms swirling in patterns, hair hanging like ropes to the floor.

"And what sacrifices are these?" The young man asked, slightly fearful, despite his resolve.

"In order to understand the mysteries of the universe, you must be willing to sacrifice everything you are now for everything that you wish to become, and everything you wish to know. You must give up your past, and your future, and live only in the now- you must even give up your name, only taking a new one when you require it, to be shed when you are finished like a snake sheds his skin. You will walk in a world of shadow and illusion, of fear and power, of darkness and light."

The young man understood what it meant to dedicate oneself to a goal, and his fear dissolved. "I am willing to make the sacrifices and become your student," he said with certainty. "What must I do after I make these sacrifices?"

"You must learn the songs of power and sing them in the deep places, using them to change the fabric of reality. You must learn to dream while waking, and walk freely between the worlds, learning secret wisdom from the spirits that dwell in them. You must learn to carve the symbols of might into the very flesh of the cosmos, and see your will twist and change it. All these things you will learn, and be transformed by them."

"I will do these things," the young man said, and set out on the path to becoming a sorceror. For the next three years, he learned the words, names and songs of power, roaring them with ferocity or singing them beautifully in the deep dark places of the earth. He drank strange mixtures of root and bark and went mad for days at a time, walking in and out of all the worlds and conversing with the spirits and demons that lived there, waking screaming and covered in sweat. He came to know the signs and carvings of time beyond reckoning, and learned the way to cut them into the body of the Great Tree of All-That-Is, twisting its branches and watching his will take form and shape and effects that went beyond even his own understanding. At the end of the three years, his mind was nearly gone from the mixtures he had taken in profusion, at times having difficulty remembering his own name, before recalling that he had no name except what he gave himself. He was half mad from the things he had seen and haunted by his walking between the worlds. The magician sought him out at the top of a great mountain, staring out into the great expanse of the sky.

"What have you learned?" The magician asked calmly.

The young man did not speak for a long time, as though he had not heard. Slowly he began to speak. "Through sacrificing all that I was for all that I thought I wished to be, I have learned that one must first know his true Will before he makes the sacrifices, or he becomes lost in a world of pain and poison, illusion and shadow. By giving up my name, I learned that a man's thought of his own identity is foolishness. He thinks that he is his name, and when that is taken away, he loses himself to fear and self-doubt because he no longer knows who he is. Through living only in the present, I lost that fear and self doubt, and learned that the past is irreversible and the future non-existent. We can only find calm and strength through being centered in the Now, and by taking a new name, I learned that we are only what we make ourselves, and that we shape our own life as we choose.

Next, as I walked the path of the magician, I learned that sound and vibration are power through Intention. They represent without explanation or reasoning, and express without the constraint of language. By walking through the worlds, I learned that this is only one shadow in a thousand-thousand, and that our attachment to this world and all the things in it is foolishness. I learned that though there are countless worlds beyond this one, that all are One, and that all are contained within us, just as we are contained within them. Through conversing with the spirits, I learned that they were only parts of myself, just as everything that exists is part of myself, and therefore the entire cosmos is made up of all one matter and substance, writ large or small. By exerting my Will and carving those signs of power into existence, I found that it was only myself that changed, but through the changing of myself and my own perception, I saw the world changed because of this. Since myself and the worlds around me are only parts of the same, it became possible for me to understand that transforming the Self and transforming the Cosmos are one idea."

The magician tilted his head back and howled with laughter that resounded through the sky. "You have learned many things, young man. But I knew when you arrived that you would not find what you were seeking here with me."

The young man nodded, and made to walk down the mountain. "Where should I look next, sorceror? I have searched in the temple, and have learned the secrets of alchemy and magic, seen the other worlds and still have not found understanding. I do not know where my footsteps should take me."

The magician looked for a long while at the young man. "There are certain things you must find in order to know what you wish."

"What are these objects, and where do I find them?"

"These objects are the Hall of Blood, the Mask of the Unfettered, the Tireless Steed, the Sword of Princes, the King's Faithful Friend, the Crown of Fire, the Rushing Wind, the Cloak of Heroes, and the Sacred Ring. I can tell you how to find them; I can speak of them, but they can only be found by someone who is willing to go forth and seek them out. They are each of them the key to a great mystery, and through them, you will at last come to your journey's end. It is through action and experience that power and understanding are gained. Have you not learned this yet?"

"I have."

"Then we shall begin with the Hall of Blood. What is it that a man has as his ancestral property, from the lowliest to the highest, but that he builds upon as he grows older, and tears down as he becomes aged?"

The young man spoke without hesitation:"A man has as his ancestral property, from the lowliest pauper to the highest noble, his own body, that he builds strong as he grows, but that becomes aged and falls into disrepair in later years."

"Correct," the magician nodded. "The Hall of the Blood is one's own body, the great temple that holds within itself all these other objects that we have discussed. Inside its walls, there is a Sacred Ring. This ring is unseen, but mighty in strength, as many things fall within its circular form and are surrounded by it."

"The Ring you speak of is the binding nature of the soul," the young man said. "This Sacred Ring acts to hold together the body, the blood, the life and the spark that animates. It is that Ring that dissipates in physical death and causes the Hall to become empty and cold and hollow."

"What you say is true. The Sacred Ring is the yoke of the soul, set in place the instant we are quickened, and remaining with us until death. When we die, it releases those things which give life to the body and allows our flesh to return to the black earth. So you see that there are many things that make us what we are, and not a simple dyad of flesh and soul."

"What more is there to a man but flesh and soul?" questioned the young man. "It would seem to me that these two things are what make the individual."

"This is because you see no difference between all the wondrous divisions that exist within one man, divisions that are all pieces of the One, just as in nature there are many divisions that are not divisions, but rather expressions of the whole. This same reason is why the fool seeks endlessly around the world for the one true god, and is so blind he cannot see that all gods are expressions of the same god. All truths are only one sliver in the Great Tree."

"What then are the further divisions that make up a man, and what forms do they take?"

"That is for you to discover. We have spoken of two, but now you must go forth, and find for yourself the other things of which we have spoken. Return to me each time you have found one."

"I will do this thing that you ask," replied the young man, and strode down from the mountain with the magician laughing quietly behind him.

For some time, he wandered aimlessly, considering the things that he had learned in his life thus far. He thought back to his time in the temple, praying and fasting and controlling his baser thoughts. He remembered the home of the alchemist, bringing forth fire from stone, and creating wondrous compounds with myriad use. His mouth went dry as his mind went to the emptiness that he had known through losing his own identity, and he laughed as he remembered the fearlessness that came from freeing oneself from the constricting ideas of form and self-deception. After walking in this fashion for days, he sat down at a crossroads and pondered all these things silently. In his silence, he found that calm that comes from living in the present and quieting the shrieking uncertainties of past and future. He listened to his own heart, and heard the sound of his breath rising and falling, and he began to reflect on it. He counted each breath for a day at a time, thinking to himself, "20,000 times I have breathed today. 20,000 shallow breaths, and I have never given mind to it before!" So he gave himself over to the study of his breathing, and lost all count of day or month. Sometimes he would inhale only once an hour, or he would match his exhalations with the falling of a leaf, gaining absolute control of it, and being overwhelmed by a feeling of peace and gratitude each time he was able to draw in air once again. He meditated on the wonderful mysteries of creation, and at the end of one such, he saw in his vision the Great Tree, and heard a sound like the beating of great wings, wings that produced a great wind to rise up and shake the leaves of the Tree, and his heart leaped in his chest as he came back from the sight.

He returned once again to the hut where the magician lived, and was greeted on the path outside by the familiar form of the old sorceror, hair like moss hanging from trees, his eye always seeming to penetrate everything around him.

"You have returned. It has been a long time since you left here, and you have grown older! What have you discovered in your absence?"

The young man looked down at himself, and marveled at the long beard that grew down his chest, his clothes long since gone to rags. He laughed at himself, and how wild he must look. "I have discovered that my breath is the Rushing Wind around the Great Tree of my body, each rising and falling a great gift given to each of us, seldom considered. I have found that through being mindful of it, sickness and death are exhaled from the body, and that strength and rejuvenation and life enter miraculously with each inhalation. I have seen that this is a beautiful thing, and something that should be known and developed by every man."

The magician inclined his head, and strode back into his shelter, leaving the young man in the gathering gloom. "Well done," he said over his shoulder. "I will see you again when you have made a new discovery."

So, the young man set out again on his journey, placing his feet one in front of the other on that path with no end. He was now conscious of his breathing each step of the way, but grew disheartened after walking his dusty way for some weeks.

"What am I looking for?" He asked himself. "What am I doing here, wandering this endless road, its great expanse as empty as I am? Have I learned anything at all, or have I merely spoken words that I hoped were true, lying to myself so that my life might appear to have some meaning?" His thoughts went in this direction for a long time, discouraging him and conquering him like a raging black river of doubt, until his anguish and agony were all he knew.

He had come all this way, these last many years, all for nothing, he told himself. Truth was just another Illusion hidden behind shadow after poisonous shadow, waiting like a mirage in the desert to mock the seeker with its dissolving visage. The young man walked through thunderstorm and dry desert, his skin cracked and burnt from the sun. He had left all civilization behind, living like a beast, forgetting the tongues of men and living off whatever he could forage. He was naked, his hair and beard tangled and matted like some wild things mane; he was savage, losing all grip on his time spent in the world of man. The priest, the alchemist and the magician seemed like some far-off, barely remembered flicker, as though thinking on a someone else's dream that he had only been told of. Deep in the forests, the young man lost his mind. Seasons came and went and he did not notice, inside his cave, staring deep into the eye sockets of some dead thing he had killed and eaten. Somewhere down inside them, a spark glimmered, and he shuddered a great wracking sob.

All at once, it was as though a fire had kindled inside of him, his entire body blazing with it from his head downward and back throughout him again, and a sky-shattering shriek tore its way from his throat. He was overtaken by the ecstasy and the madness of being alive, a living creature in a world of dead, grey ghosts. What a feeling overtook him! He danced wildly, flailing his limbs and leaping through the trees- he could feel all the life pulsing in the world around him, each rock and root, stump and stick, bird and bone, all coursing with their own energy, feeding him and feeding from him in a terrible and wondrous symbiosis. Each second lasted a thousand years, his blood roaring through the veins as though it would burst from his body and spray the very moon with his essence. He ran, and continued to run throughout the night, and then day followed and melted into darkness again before he slowed. His footsteps took on purpose once again as his mind slowly returned to him, images coming together like fragments of broken pottery, each one a word or face or fleeting moment. Without considering where he was or where he was going, he arrived at the home of the magician once more.

He walked past the piles of skulls and crossed the threshold where the door hung open, crossing the floor to the pallet where the old man slept. He shook the sorceror by the arm, but he did not wake. His eye stared sightlessly at the smoke-hole in the roof. The man, who was no longer young, closed his eye with one hand and addressed the corpse.

"I return to you again, wise one. I have learned much and come back from the wilderness of despair and madness with three of the things you spoke to me of. Through anguish and agony, I lost myself and lost my way, living as a beast in the forest for many years. I had no concept of time or space, and forgot the languages of man and god, surviving in a cave like a starving wolf. But after many winters in the blackness, I stared deep into the eyes of death and considered the truths that I saw there.

At once, I realized one of the great mysteries of the universe, and attained the Crown of Fire: that blazing thing which outshines the sun is the madness and frenzy that pours in through the skull, setting one aflame with the fire of life. It is the ecstatic state of creation and destruction, of rage and fear, of the supreme boundless joy of living and the utter desolation of pure and total death.

As it filled me completely, I saw to the edges of All That Is, and beyond. I became light and darkness, cruelty and mercy and all other things that are now and ever have been, and I knew what it is to be god. Upon these realizations, my mind returned to me, and I regained my powers of thought and reason- these are the dual edges of what you named the Sword of Princes- for a prince among men wields his mind the way a soldier wields a deadly sword, and he he has the understanding that in the hands of one who has honed it well, the Sword of Princes is deadlier than any weapon man could ever create.

And as my mind returned, I saw my memories coming back to me like the shards of a great vase dashed into a thousand thousand pieces, and my experiences gave me comfort and wisdom. I came to know that this is what was meant by the King's Faithful Friend. For a king among men, his most trusted friend must be his own memory and experiences. A man who must put his faith in the words of another will often find himself in sorrow and ruin. And like a fully loyal friend, one must earn that counsel through the deeds of a lifetime that he can turn back to in remembrance when in need.

But now you, my old teacher, are dead and gone, and I must now look to myself to finish this journey that you have set me on."

The man then lifted the body of his teacher up, and carried him outside, where he prepared a pyre of wood and oil and sweet-smelling incenses. He laid the body atop it, and considered the face of the magician, who seemed to be smiling a slight smile. "You have seen the mysteries, and death held no fear for you, old man, as it no longer holds any for me." The man set the torch to the oil, somberly, slowly- in reverence. The flames licked the sky, with a hunger he knew, and he sang in a strong voice words of sending and returning, the songs of eternal rebirth- being, becoming, fading away, and being reborn again. He threw his head back and laughed a laugh of great joy and love for the old man, and stayed awake staring into the ashes until long after the fire had gone to sleep, placing the blackened skull with the others at the doorway of the hut.

His path became clear to him, and he re-entered the hut and lay down on the magicians bed, saying: "I am now you, old man."

So for years that followed, he lived in the hut and conversed with the skulls of all the magicians that had gone before him, and spoke words of transformation to the young men that came to seek him, just as he had done so long before. He knew that he had put on the Mask of the Unfettered; by separating himself from the idea that he was bound by his own persona, he came to the realization that he was every persona- he only needed to slip the mask on and become what he would for as long as he chose, shattering the single strand of his being into myriad threads, watching each one weave and twist and spiral their way to a greater destiny.

He lived seldom in the world of illusion and flesh that surrounded him, choosing rather to remain in long periods of meditation, sometimes simply breathing and thinking of nothing at all. At other times he would send himself out on what he came to know as the Tireless Steed, traversing the worlds at will, or visiting places far away and outside the foolish ideas of time that most men concern themselves with. He laughed to himself when he realized that this was all but one of the objects he had been sent to find those many years ago, when he was still a young man. So, one day, while conversing with an apprentice, he stood and put a hand on the young man's shoulder in blessing, bestowing the small shelter on him with a smile, and strode out of the forest that he had called home for so long. As he walked, his long, long hair and beard flowed out in the wind around him, and it seemed to him that all the many deeds of his long, long life danced together in the air around him and the space within him like a flock of many colored birds. They flew and turned and rose and fell in a beautiful pattern, and finally wove themselves together to cover him in a Cloak of Heroes.

As he thought of the twisted ways that had led him here, the men he had studied with and learned from, and all the words they had spoken to him, the faces of the priest, the alchemist, the magician and himself all melted together into one, and he laughed as each footstep followed the other on a path with no end.

***

The magician set out along the road, covered now by the magnificent Cloak of Heroes, and possessing all those Nine Objects that he had been told to seek out. His understanding dawned slowly with each step that only now could he come to any sort of focus on this path he had been walking. His error in the years of youth had been that he sought first the Mysteries without, and had no sense of the Mysteries within-through knowing little and less of himself, his being, all the pieces that made him One, he had been like a wanderer in the desert; not knowing where he was, or where he was headed, nor knowing that on his person existed a map to find his way, a skin of water to drink from, and a tent with which to find shade in the blazing heat of the midday sun.

He only smiled and shook his head at his own foolishness, then allowed it to slip away like a feather in the wind, forgiving himself and doing away with the idea entirely. Before long, his road led him back into a city, the dust rising up in great clouds from the feet and wagon wheels of people from many nations. For some time, he allowed himself to be swept away with the throng, being jostled this way and that by a thousand different faces, voices, and bodies, forming a rushing river of desire and striving. Each and every person that made up the river was overwhelmed by their own sense of importance, none of them noticing that they were only one tiny droplet in this roaring mass of humanity. All were isolated and alone even as they were surrounded by the crowds, for all were convinced of their separateness from one another and all things around them; they were blinded by their own sense of self, lost in the choking black shadow of loneliness and fear. Finally, he separated himself from the writhing masses, breathing a great breath of freedom and relief as his whole being disentangled itself from the fray.

Looking about, the magician saw that he was in a marketplace of wondrous size, sellers and merchants of all color and tongue offering anything that the mind could conceive in their stalls and wagons and · silken pavilions. His eyes were filled with splendor and variety, the music of a thousand instruments and the cries of a thousand hawkers screaming their wares; all about him were sights of unspeakable beauty and variation, so that he became overwhelmed by them, entranced by each new trinket or dancer or singing bird that he came to. His mind ran to overflowing with nothing but the contents of the marketplace, and he soon forgot his great journey and the things he was seeking, those having been replaced by a million things and ideas he would never have dreamed real.

Reclining inside a tent, he filled his lungs with opiate smoke, watching a young girl move and sway sinuously to the music of hypnotic pipe and drum. Another woman washed and brushed his hair and cut his beard to make him appear more attractive and civilized in the common fashion, perfuming his body and dressing him in fine robes. The ease of it all was so comforting, he soon closed his eyes from the weight of the drug and the drink and the drowsiness that came over him after indulging all his senses in a world he had never known. He slept and he slept, awaking for brief periods of time to wander the marketplace until returning to the silk tent with the women and the smoke and the hot, fiery liquor that burned his throat and put his disquiet to rest. Sometimes he would remember an image, or experience a brief dissatisfaction with his actions, a quiet but desperate yearning for something only barely remembered, hovering there at the edge of his dreams, just underneath the seductive songs of the dark eyed women surrounding him. When those moments came, he struggled to grasp them wholly, to remember who he was, what it was that had brought him here and where he had been going before the marketplace, but he could not remember.

His body grew soft and his mind softer, the Hall falling into disrepair and the Sword growing dull and tarnished. His Faithful Friend had been sent away, and now he could not rely on him for counsel. The Crown had been nearly extinguished, its once blazing fire now a faint flickering that threatened to fail any moment, and the Tireless Steed was lost to him. The Cloak had become a pitiful, threadbare thing in bad need of repair and upkeep and the Mask had broken in pieces, leaving him trapped and unaware of his ability to shape himself in any way he saw fit. The Rushing Wind was a shallow breath, now, and he had long forgotten the way he had sat at the crossroads aware of every inhalation being a willful act to Live. The Ring was weak.

One day as the magician walked the marketplace, seeking some new diversion to take his mind away from the growing feeling of despair that had taken hold of him lately, his gaze fell on a youngster begging in the shade of an awning that offered some slight respite from the day's heat. The boy was thin, one leg splayed out beside him, and his alms-bowl was cracked and empty; yet there was a fire in his eyes that the magician could see, and recognized for what it was. The boy's open, fearless countenance reminded him of himself, of who he was and who he had been as a young man, seeking the mysteries and preparing himself for the Great Journey.

He approached the boy, and seated himself nearby. He watched the lad for a time, seeing how he could not make any money through begging because of his fierce countenance, and the way that the numb crowd avoided him and his fiery eyes. There was an accusation there in those eyes, damning the masses even as he lived at the edge of the crowd, one of them and yet not one of them, uncertain of how to remove himself, yet despising them for not accepting him as one of their own.

"I can see that you are in difficult circumstance," said the magician to the young man softly. "And that you are in need of assistance. I can offer this assistance, if you would have it."

The boy eyed him mistrustfully. "What assistance, and why would you offer it? I am a cripple, and a beggar, starving here in the marketplace. You appear to be a wealthy man of means, and I have often seen you walking the market drunk or drugged with beautiful women at your side."

The magician smiled. "I am a simple traveler who has become lost in distraction. My clothing and intoxication and company are all a part of the snare that this place has laid for me; it gives you many fine and wondrous things until you become used to them, dependent on them. Then it lays your debts on the scales, and enslaves you to work for these things for the rest of your life- but by then, the things that you have been given no longer provide you with joy, so you must always find new diversions, deepening your debt and enslavement. In many ways, it is you, the beggar, who has nothing but his bowl, that is the free man- all these that you see here are the true beggars and slaves."

"It is easy for a man with everything to speak so to one who has nothing," said the young man, his voice full of venom and weariness.

"I have lost everything in this place. I, who began my journey with nothing, became wealthy though I wore rags and had no home to live in, or food to eat. But here, I have become a beggar in spirit, having lost all the wealth that I gained in my travels." The magician gestured to his robes and bracelets. "These outer trappings are the symbols of inner poverty."

The boy laughed in scorn. "Then give me your poverty, so that I might sell it. I would welcome what you call hardship!"

"Gladly," answered the magician, tossing his bracelets and rings into the beggar's bowl, removing his robes and laying them in the dust, until he stood in his undergarment, laughing.

"Why do you laugh," asked the boy, confused and wondering at this strange man's actions.

"I laugh because I feel as though a great weight has fallen from my shoulders, and a blindfold from my eyes. I remember who I am, and where I was going before I came to this place, and that has filled me with a sense of joy, and so I laugh at my own stupidity and carelessness."

"Who are you then?" asked the boy. "And where are you going?"

"Who I am is less important than where I am going. The who changes constantly, like watching a flock of birds fly and disperse and regroup itself into new formation, or watching a tree grow from sapling to giant- what makes it what it is? What makes a man what he is, other than the journey he undertakes in his life? What we are is what we choose to be, but it is of great importance that we make this choice from a place of understanding where it is that we are meant to go. If a man chooses a life that is not in harmony with his own destiny, he will fail in that life, either through insufficiency or dissatisfaction. Therefore, he must spend the first part of his journey understanding himself completely, and in this way will come to know where his true path lies."

"But how does one know oneself in this way," asked the young man, his eyes burning even more strongly than before. "I have lost use of one of my legs, and my journey, it seems, ends there. How can I journey towards my goal if I am incomplete? It was my intention to come here to this city and make something of myself, until I injured myself working the fields. Now I am destined to be a beggar, for what can I do, how can I make myself something great when I am a cripple with no means for a living or way to survive? Am I not trapped by the circumstances that made me this way?"

"You are trapped only by your perception. You may still make something of yourself, but the question is only what will you make yourself become with the tools that you have available? Applying yourself in the way that you did before you injured your leg is pointless, but now you must find a way to apply yourself in a new way that takes your current self into consideration. Your anger and despair stems from the expectations and desires that you had before you lost your legs, and now that you have lost them, you dwell in the shadow of those former desires, at the mercy of them as they hold you under the current of misery and despondency.

If you were poor for many years, basing all your decisions on those circumstances that you were in as a poor man, and then one day you became rich, would you not then change your method of living and process of decision-making in order to match your difference in means? Just as this is true, so it is true that we not become enmeshed and ensnared by who we were, but be ever-conscious of who we are at our current stage of being, making our decisions and basing our growth from the present, not the past. Likewise, despair comes either from living in the past, or living in the unmanifest future, where lies only uncertainty and terror."

"What am I to do then?" The beggar asked. "For I have no skill in any craft, nor any great knowledge of the written word, the sciences or the stars. I have only my bowl and these things you have bestowed on me."

"No, my friend," said the magician solemnly. "You have the will, and the ability to use it. Come with me, and together we will find your destiny, traveling together until our paths diverge and you have become complete."

So the beggar set down his bowl, the magician took him upon his back, and together they left the marketplace with all its swirling colors and falsities.

"Where will we go?" asked the young man. "For we have nowhere to stay, and crippled as I am, I cannot walk forever. "

"We will travel until we come to a place that we can build. In that place we shall construct our Lodge, and there we will begin our work."

They were silent then for a long time, each lost in his own thoughts, the magician calmly setting one foot in front of the other, out of the city and into the vast countryside. They walked in this fashion for a long time before the magician spoke. "You see now that every single weary mile that we have walked has brought us closer to where we are attempting to arrive. Even though we do not fully know where our final step will take us, we are aware of what we are trying to achieve. In this fashion, we can compare our current endeavor to the our life's endeavor, the Great Journey. Each single movement and action we undertake must be towards that greatness. When we breathe, we must be conscious that it is a willful action to remain alive and continue on our way; when we eat, it must be to fortify our strength so that we might not lose heart or vitality along the path. This road that we walk requires our full being, our entire presence. We cannot treat it with frivolity or light words- it is a sacred and holy thing that we are doing, and must be treated as such, and every moment we draw breath must be a studied action laden with Intent and Presence."

"Is there no room then for light-heartedness and laughter in this life, then?" asked the young man.

"There is. Through following one's true path, he gains a calm and a joy that lightens his load and calls forth great laughter and a surging love of life. If these things were not present in one's life, he would know it to be empty of true meaning and purpose- if we have no love, and no joy, what is worth doing?"

After saying this, the magician himself laughed long and fully, his joy illuminating the valley around them. "You see? Even in contemplating joy and purpose, we have found our destination! Here we shall build."

They both looked about the valley, considering its rocks and its trees, feeling the rich earth under their feet and washing the dirt that streaked their bodies in the cold, clean river that ran through it. For a time, they merely sat in enjoyment of it, studying its every aspect and finding it beautiful and perfect in every way. The only sound was the peaceful river winding its way beside them, flowing gracefully over rock and root.

"I came from a place like this," the young man said, "before I sought out the city. I had never realized how much I missed the peaceful quiet of the countryside, and how filthy and loud the city around you can become. Returning now to this peacefulness and washing myself in the river has given me a silence within, and I feel clean again."

"The purity you feel comes from distancing yourself from the anger and despair, washing away your past fears and filthiness in the cleansing waters of rebirth. That beggar that you were within the confines of the city and the confines of your own perception is now gone, and you are free to begin discovering and shaping who you choose to be," said the magician. "Now you must decide where to begin building, and how."

"But I am no architect!" exclaimed the young man. "I haven't the first idea how to build with stone or wood. How am I to build a structure to house us without the knowledge?"

"The knowledge comes from the doing, and the doing comes from the intention. If your intention is pure, then so will be action. Have no concern over the outcome of what you have set forth to do- only concern yourself with doing it, and thereby whatever the accomplishment brings, you will have succeeded in achieving your goal, for it was merely to do. As you set out to build this structure, in the doing, you will come to understand many things."

The young man nodded, and looked about. "What shall we use to begin building? There is stone, there is wood, there is mud from the river and grasses in the field. With so many materials at hand, the choice is difficult where to begin!"

"Begin wherever you will," replied the magician. "Use whatever material comes to hand at first. If it is not the right material for what you are trying to build, it will show itself as such through failure. If it fails to produce the proper result, then you must change your material, or the way in which you apply it until success occurs. Do not be discouraged when such a failure happens- it is not your failure as a builder! It is merely that you applied either the improper material, or the improper method required to make use of it. This is a wondrous part of the process, and with it comes the knowledge that anything can be applied as a material, and any different kind of method can be paired with it, but that in a given situation, the knowledge of what material and what method are correct is tantamount to achieving one's goal, whatever that may be.

So, as you consider your materials, consider too what ways they may be applied. For in nature, everything flows into everything else, and there is nothing that is not a part of this connection. Therefore, be observant of the things around you, here in this valley, for they may be applied to the smallest rock or the furthest star in the heavens!"

"You speak of a stone as though it holds as much importance in the world as does a star! How can this be true, since the stone is but a tiny and base material, yet the star is burning in the firmament countless miles away, running its own course and affecting all things around it with its light and other fathomless qualities?" The young man cried in disbelief and confusion.

"The stone is small, and yet it carries within its form many of the great secrets of the universe. It can be made to affect the world around it in many ways. I can use it as a weapon to end a man's life, or begin a war. It can be used to build a house or destroy one, to grind grain into flour or bring down game. Are not all these things of great effect? Each thing is only one part of a whole, but as such, each small thing can be used to better understand a greater, just as gaining the knowledge of how to read allows a man to gain the knowledge of anything he can read. So to learn these little lines on a page can give a man the understanding of architecture, alchemy, the movements of those stars that before we called "fathomless". Then by learning these skills, a man could then build a temple, brew a poison, predict a great shift in the planets. What then would be the effects of those things on the world around him? Great, and many! You see, each tiny thing leads to a greater thing. Each word to another word, and each deed to another deed- So it is with nature and the cosmos- each thing can be seen to correspond and react to all others. Such is the wonder of this universe!"

The magician stood. "So now, we build, with a pure intention, this Lodge."

They worked tirelessly, discussing as they went the application and importance of each material, the interconnectedness of each one of them, and how best they might use it. From the ground, they decided to build a foundation of stone. "Since, as a man just learning who he is," the magician said, "you must work upward from a strong base. The rock is your spirit, sturdy and unyielding to the elements sent against it. It must be built up through hardship and constant work, therefore, we will bring each rock up from the lowest part of the valley, unearthing each one at a time. Since a man must know himself thoroughly, you will name each rock that we use, and be able to name it every day that we build further. As you will name them after strengths and virtues that you, yourself wish to have, you will spend each day, in the time that we are not building, meditating on those virtues and strengths, and how you can bring them to bear in your life now."

"I will do these things," said the young man earnestly, and he was true to his word. Ignoring his crippled leg, he worked diligently and well, naming each stone as he brought it up the hill and placed it in the foundation. He spent long hours meditating on those things he had named them, and as the weeks went by, his countenance began to change. His body grew muscled, and his gaze was clear, still full of fire, but devoid of the anger that had poisoned it in the city. The crippled leg became less of an inconvenience the more he grew accustomed to it, and soon it troubled him little, as he simply accepted it not as a limitation, but as a part of his own materials. He worked with it, and applied it in the proper way, giving little consideration to how he used to desire it to be whole again, and by the time the foundation was finished, he had taken many of the strengths after which he named the stones within himself.

After finishing the stonework, the magician and the young man stood side by side considering their work, well pleased with what they had accomplished. "What must we do next, in order to raise the structure and place a roof on it?" asked the young man.

"The pillars that support the Lodge must be strong as well. We will use the trunks of great trees to make the supports, and as you are man who has begun to shape himself, you will shape the wood into works of art. These carvings will be scenes of events that you wish to accomplish with your life, and as you carve each one, you will begin to see your destiny unfold. While carving them, think on how all the strengths and virtues you have named will be put to use during the events you are shaping."

"I will do so," said the young man. For the following months, he felled trees with stone axes, forming the framework of the Lodge, his hands growing rough and callused. The beams were sunk and set, and the walls made of hewn plank, each board known and placed one at a time. After he had set all the pillars, he studied them for a long while, his hands running over them, feeling their smoothness and texture, the grain and beauty that lay within each one. Some while later, he began to carve them, first here and now there, standing back for a long while, or sitting deep in meditation before moving on to the next one. The magician merely sat quietly and watched him, studying each carving as it began to reach completion, occasionally smiling, or nodding his head, sometimes laughing quietly to himself.

When each piece was fully realized, the young man set down his chisel and hammer, and looked at each one in turn.

"What have you learned of yourself in carving the pillars?" inquired the magician.

"When I began shaping them, I spent quite some time in meditation on what I truly desired in life, and then I began. But each deed that I carved seemed as though I had accomplished it already, and the strands of time began to thread in and out of each other. I saw my life as it could be in a thousand different ways, as a carpenter and a husband, as a teacher and an artist. I lived these lives as I shaped them, knowing their joys and sorrows, their cares and triumphs, knowing each one intimately as I lost myself in the work. I carved all these deeds that I could fit onto each one of these wooden columns, but each one is only a possibility of what could become. As I finished, I began to see what their common ties were: they were all of them possible, because each one of them or all of them can be open to me if I so choose it. I am free to shape myself even as I shaped these pieces of wood, in any way I see fit, seeking out those things in life that are my desire, and changing, reshaping, constantly growing and creating anew, not bound by the chains of circumstance, for I am free to alter that circumstance and change my environment. I am both hammer and anvil, smith and metal, forging and being forged by my own actions and art. I shape my own life."

"It is just as you say," said the magician.

"What now?" asked the young man.

The magician laughed. "You require only a roof to complete the Lodge. What is it that this will teach you?"

The young man considered. "If the foundation is the indomitable nature of spirit, and the pillars represent the strength of will to create our own destiny, what is the roof but a completion of the structure? Man raising himself up to his highest point and remaining there in perfect balance with the rest of the pieces that join together to form a whole. The apex of existence can only be discovered through this strong foundation and this pure will to create ourselves in harmony with the natural laws of the universe."

"You are ready, then to finish this work that you have begun," said the magician. The young man fell to.

When the roof was completed, the two stood side by side again. "It is completed, then," said the young man.

"It is," agreed the magician. "What does its completion mean to you?"

"That every act of intention and completion makes each of us a mighty magician in our own right. We are free to alter and construct our own reality, not as a fool or a coward, who would deceive himself by either running from the truth or telling himself it is as he wishes; but as a strong and powerful being, capable of creating real change in his life, his surroundings, his universe, by recognizing himself as an artist whose tool is Will. Through this simple realization, each individual can attain illumination, fulfillment, contentment, merely by discovering their goal and attaining it."

The magician nodded very slowly, then laid his hand on the young man's shoulder. "You are ready to live your life, recognizing yourself as a magician, one who shapes himself and the world through first purifying and strengthening and knowing his innermost being, and then using that knowledge as the material which he will apply through the method of will." He clapped his hands sharply, once.

Around them, the valley began to fade and change, the Lodge dissolved, the trees, the river, the grasses, all were replaced by the din of the marketplace, its colors and its madness and its crowds. Both magician and young man sat still in the dust, ignoring the distraction and the chaos. The young man smiled, and the magician laughed, and slowly walked once more from the marketplace.

Acknowledgements

Thanks go out to all those who have supported this endeavor in any way, with special mention going out to the following:

Justin B.
Michael G.
Ron D.
Johannes F.
Dylan C.

www.operationwerewolf.com

Printed in Great Britain
by Amazon

33199210R00076